The AMERICAN CENTURY Series

SEEKONK
IN THE TWENTIETH CENTURY

THE AMERICAN CENTURY SERIES

SEEKONK

IN THE TWENTIETH CENTURY

Phyllis A. Dupere

ARCADIA

First published 1997
Copyright © Phyllis A. Dupere, 1997

ISBN 0-7524-0923-9

Published by Arcadia Publishing,
an imprint of the Chalford Publishing Corporation,
One Washington Center, Dover, New Hampshire 03820.
Printed in Great Britain

Library of Congress Cataloging-in-Publication Data applied for

Contents

Acknowledgments

This pictorial book was created to reflect on a century of change and growth within the town of Seekonk, Massachusetts. Images obtained while viewing photographs from varied private and public collections were selected to illustrate the best and worst of times. Whether through celebrations, accidents, or storms, townspeople came together not only for each occasion but also for each other.

Numerous thanks go out to those businesses and townspeople who so graciously assisted me in the formation of this book:

Louise Oakland, Mary DaSilva, Frank Mooney, William Saleeba, Dr. Jared Stubbs, Wallace Guay, Mark Chandler of Country Kitchen, Lois McDonald of Leonard's Antiques, the family of the late Nelson B. Stackpole, the John Wolstencroft family, the Seekonk School Department, the Seekonk Public Library, Stephen Leavitt and Ronald Charron of the Seekonk Police Department, the Oliver Hopkins Jr. family, Irving Dickens of Belwing Turkey Farm, Dr. Raymond George, Robert DelRosso, Rev. David Marquard of the Faith Christian Center, and those who provided me with leads and contacts.

Special thanks go to RJB for his assistance in this endeavor. Without these people, there would be no book.

Any omissions of people, places, or events in this publication were not done intentionally.

Introduction

Settled in 1636, the town of Seekonk, Massachusetts, assumed its name from the Native American words "Seaki," meaning black, and "Honk," meaning goose, referring to the wild geese that frequented the Seekonk River and its cove during their semiannual migrations. Other variations of the spelling of the town's name ranged from Secunk, or Seconch, to Squannakonk. Tales of how Seekonk received its name also vary; however, the majority of them refer to the geese that settled in the area.

From 1645 to 1812, Seekonk was included as a small portion of the old town of Rehoboth, Massachusetts, a land tract purchase from Massasoit, a member of the Wampanoag tribe, in 1641. On February 26, 1812, Seekonk, retaining its original name, incorporated into a separate, distinct township in the Commonwealth of Massachusetts.

The first town meeting was called to order less than a month later on Monday, March 16, 1812, at 10 am. At that meeting, Caleb Abell was chosen moderator and town clerk with Captain Allen Cole as treasurer. A week later, three selectmen were chosen—Peter Hunt, Worcester Carpenter, and Allen Monroe.

This new town had two distinct villages: Pawtucket, in the northwestern parcel bordering the Blackstone River; and Seekonk, more centrally located on the banks of the Ten Mile River and Seekonk River. Within the span of sixteen years, they grew apart, with Pawtucket finally forming its own new town on March 17, 1828. By a United States Supreme Court decree dated March 1, 1862, Seekonk lost its western sector to Rhode Island and that piece of land became the town of East Providence. In exchange, the Rhode Island town of Fall River was deeded to Massachusetts.

At the October 1, 1812 town meeting, $350 was voted for support of the district schools for one year, with a total town budget of $1,600. By 1900, after struggling with a major population and land loss in 1862, the town budget was nearing $20,000. In 1997, schools received proceeds totaling $14.8 million for renovation of the middle school and the Aitken Elementary School. The 1998 annual town budget was set at $22,508,618.

Farming was the principal occupation of the early settlers in the area for many years, until the power of the Seekonk and Ten Mile Rivers was recognized in the late 1700s. Textile and gristmills sprang up along the river banks. In 1862, when the majority of this portion of "original Seekonk" was transferred to East Providence, Rhode Island,

Seekonk was once again dependent upon its agricultural background.

By 1905, the population was approximately 1,917. As the years passed, the population grew slowly. By the late 1950s, Seekonk became known as a suburban, bedroom community, and its population jumped to 8,399 in the 1960 census. Its current population of 13,046 is down slightly from the projected amount due to an unexpected number of families moving out of town and deaths.

Situated in Bristol County, Massachusetts, Seekonk is a long and narrow town, spanning a distance over 11 miles in length from north to south, but only about 2 miles in width from east to west, covering a total area of 18.63 square miles. The town is divided into three fire districts and three voting precincts.

Baker's Corner at the junction of Newman Avenue, Central Avenue, and Pine Street in the North End and Luther's Corner at Fall River Avenue and County Street in the South End were major population and shopping districts for years. These two regions were separated by the ledge, rocks, and hilly land of Central Seekonk, which itself is intersected by Routes 44 and 114A. With the building of Interstate Route 195 through South Seekonk in the late 1950s, the Route 6 area in the extreme southern end of town has evolved into the shopping and business zone of the 1990s, while residential developments sprouted from former farmlands in other areas of town.

In 1997, Seekonk still has its geese, although now they are mostly Canada geese who are year-round inhabitants of local ponds. The town continues to change it appearance as renovations are made to older buildings and new structures are built. Through the images in this book, Seekonk hopefully will be long remembered as a town that grew with strength from its deep roots of community.

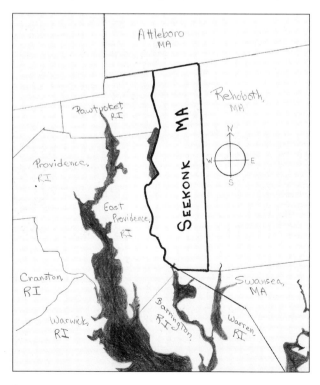

A map of Seekonk and vicinity.

One
Neighborhoods: Homes and Streets

With Seekonk being long and narrow, three communities of differing personalities emerged from within the borders of one town. The North End was influenced by both the cities of Attleboro, Massachusetts, and Pawtucket, Rhode Island. South Seekonk was the shopping and business district. Central Seekonk was regarded as a farming and residential area. All share a common thread that unites them: these neighborhoods started out with loving families extending concern for those around them. In this picture, Mrs. Louise DaSilva, a proud mother and wife of a farmer, sits on the stoop of her County Street home in 1908, surrounded by her five daughters: Mary (her first-born), Isabel (the youngest), Louise, Christina, and Madeline (in foreground).

A skating party held on one of the many ponds in Seekonk brings a group of neighborhood children together in the winter of 1900. The chaperons keep an eye out for their safety.

In the fall of 1909, with firewood chopped and stacked out back, a Seekonk resident takes time out to chat with a friend (in the suit) who dropped by for a visit from Newport, Rhode Island, for the day.

The Bradley Homestead, located on Walker Street, was surrounded by a white picket fence in 1913. Members of the family sat out on the porch to enjoy the cooling afternoon shade from the large tree in front of their home.

Lined with trees along the way, this dirt road was highly traveled in 1914. Prospect Street was wide enough for a horse and buggy to easily journey from one farm to the other.

County Street was one of the major roads in town back in 1915. A gentleman directs his horse down the winding, dirt street on his way to visit an acquaintance.

At the corner of Arcade and Fall River Avenues in the mid-1920s, traffic was not very congested. Note that cars were parked in the island while the owners got grain ground at the Grist Mill.

Luther's Corner had trolley car tracks coming up lower County Street from East Providence, Rhode Island, and turning right, heading south onto telegraph pole-lined Fall River Avenue. The curved tracks are located in the bottom right-hand corner of this 1919 photograph. Some patrons of the shops arrived this way, but others came by bicycle to pick up their goods.

An old dam on the north side of the present Newman Avenue spills over into the Ten Mile River. This is how it looked in the 1920s, almost fifteen years before the reservoir project was completed.

The five DaSilva girls, now in their teens and early twenties, are joined by their brother Richmond, wearing a sailor's suit, and their mother (standing, second from left) in the summer of 1924.

14

These bicycle-riding buddies in the early 1930s were William Sloane of Field Street and Milton Dupuoy of Newman Avenue. They are taking a break after cruising around the neighborhood. During World War II, Milton's plane was lost in the Pacific.

Sitting near the Japanese Iris flower beds on the side of the house, a young mother and her children enjoy a quiet moment together on a late spring day in 1937.

Seekonk was inundated with heavy rains and strong winds during the September 22, 1938 hurricane, creating added work for the annual fall cleanup. Luckily for the owner, this car escaped the storm (and the tree) with no damages. Most Seekonk property owners suffered tree downage from the storm, but there was little in the way of structural damage, although those few that did get hit, got hit brutally.

A large tree which uprooted in the front of this home during the '38 Hurricane has already had its limbs sawed off. One tree of this size produced an abundance of firewood for the woodpile out back. Despite the extra work that the downed tree brought, no damage was done to the house. The worst problem was that it was only one of many trees that fell on the property during the severe storm.

Cumberland Farms Dairy Store was the place to go in the 1940s if you needed an extra quart of milk or a loaf of bread. The family's station wagon was the way to get there.

During 1945, Yankee Diner at Baker's Corner was a favorite breakfast or lunch stop for truckers on Newman Avenue. A trailer from Standard Transportation Co., Inc. stands at the corner. An arrowed sign on the telephone pole indicates the direction of Fall River, Massachusetts (one would head toward the diner).

A fallen tree during the 1954 hurricane severely dented this automobile. All parts of Seekonk spent weeks picking up debris from trees downed and repairing roofs that were damaged by the storm.

Summer at McHale's (Sand and Gravel Company) Pit was the place to be in 1956. Two brave souls are about to jump into the cool, refreshing water from a homemade diving board.

Route 6 in Seekonk was the main highway going from Rhode Island to any other location in southeastern Massachusetts or Cape Cod. In 1959, weeping willow trees graced Highland Avenue, slightly east of the East Providence line.

The corner of Anthony Street and Route 6 (Fall River Avenue) was dotted with small shops and businesses. Gulf and Esso gasoline stations provided shoppers with fuel for their cars without having to cross over the busy intersection in 1959.

In an explosion heard all the way to Boston on the snowy night of January 12, 1964, Thompson Chemical Company went up in flames. Houses near the plant in the North End felt the effects the most with thick smoke, numerous broken windows, and frozen water pipes.

Neighborhood children met at the Wolstencroft home on Jean Drive to build a lemonade stand on a sultry, summer day in August 1986. The street is located in the Briarwood section of town.

Growth of a neighborhood continues on Read Street with the construction of this new house during the summer of 1997. Dr. Raymond George Jr. and his wife, Dr. Debra Williams George, both local orthodontists with offices located at the Pine Grove Professional Center on Taunton Avenue, will be enjoying their new residence for years to come. More new homes are also being built in the surrounding area.

Two
Workplaces:
Business and Industry

Seekonk has many small businesses and restaurants owned and operated by townspeople, but larger chain stores are gradually infiltrating the community. Many patrons appreciated that the store owner greeted them by name and that they could put the purchase "on their tab," not a credit card, and pay for it at a later date. In this picture, Lambert Hardware at Baker's Corner provided an assortment of nails and other hardware for do-it-yourselfers and contractors in the area. In March 1950, nails were commonly found in bins, and the customer bought them by the pound. The nails were wrapped up in brown paper torn from the roll.

The Grist Mill, owned by Moses A. Smith from 1895 to 1918, operated as a gristmill and sawmill. Moses had bought the business from his wife's father, who ran the establishment prior to 1895. Smith leased out the icehouse business to the Mellen family.

Parkinson Bros. Grain Store was located at Luther's Corner during the 1900s. Customers would arrive in horse-drawn vehicles on a weekly basis to pick up the necessary supplies for the farm.

By 1933, the Grist Mill was taken over by Louis D. Martin, a cousin of Rachel Ellen Smith (Moses' wife). The slogan over the door read: "We have good grist on hand to grind and keep the mill a going."

Leavitt's General Store, c. 1930s, on Taunton Avenue sold just about anything you would need for the home. There was a gas pump out front, also. The store has undergone slight renovations over the years and is now home to Country Kitchen, a restaurant.

A Socony gas station in 1938 awaits a customer at 85 Newman Avenue, across the street from Hibbert's store. The air whistle, the tall dark shape on the left corner of the station, is the fire alarm whistle for the volunteer fire department.

A popular eatery in South Seekonk was Eileen Darling's. Numerous wedding and anniversary parties were held in the Martha Washington Room of the restaurant. In 1950, a 50th wedding anniversary party took place for Joseph and Louise DaSilva.

Seekonk Fire Co. No. 1 was in action, responding to the 1950 fire call from the Hearthstone Restaurant. Later, the restaurant relocated to Taunton Avenue. Eventually, the land and building were sold to Johnson & Wales College, now Johnson & Wales University.

The Grist Mill Gift Shop and Bakery, adjacent to the Grist Mill restaurant, welcomed visitors in the early 1950s with unique gifts for the home and alluring aromas from the kitchen. Behind the shop were peacocks, who displayed their brilliant plumage to all.

Murgo's Barber Shop with its striped pole on the facade of the red brick building was a busy place, especially on Saturdays in 1951. Many local residents frequented the shop on a weekly basis, keeping their tresses trimmed. Located slightly south of Luther's Corner on Fall River Avenue, the building still stands, only now it houses a beauty parlor on one side and a pager business on the other.

Kinnane's Drug Store had two different addresses on Fall River Avenue at Luther's Corner (County Street). In 1951, the drug store was located on the easterly side of the road. Later, the store moved directly across the street into the spot once occupied by Parkinson Bros. Grain Store and an IGA grocery store. The building is now the home of State Line Convenient Store.

In the North End of Seekonk, Lambert Hardware had a large clientele. The building was later expanded to include the Greenbriar Gift Shop and J.E. Brennan Drug Store, becoming one of the first strip malls of the 1950s on Central Avenue.

Both the Jolly Miller Club in 1957 and the Nottingham Village Complex in 1968 were across the pond from the Old Grist Mill Restaurant. The same building, though greatly renovated, currently houses Vinny's Antiques Center.

An Esso Servicenter and Tastee-Freeze Ice Cream Shop stood at the corner of Pleasant Street and Taunton Avenue in 1959. Since then the gas station has been torn down, and Don Mills Models resides there. Sundaes is the name of the ice cream stand.

The Falstaff Restaurant and Cocktail Lounge was located on Route 6 in South Seekonk, across the street from Eileen Darling's in 1958. It has changed hands throughout the years; in 1983 it was called Brillo's, and since the mid-1990s it has been known as the Bugaboo Creek Steakhouse.

One of the more interesting restaurants during the late 1950s and early 1960s was the Pink Elephant on Route 44. Carhops (waitresses) took your meal order from your car window. Food was delivered on a tray which attached to the car window. You paid for your food upon arrival. When it was time to leave, you put your headlights on to attract your carhop's attention to remove the tray and its trash.

Walter's Market and the Seekonk branch of the National Bank of Attleboro shared the same North End building in this 1970 scene. At the meat market, one could choose the cut of meat wanted from the display case. If the customer did not see the cut of meat that he or she wanted in the case, the butcher would go into the meat locker to select and cut a piece to order.

Stanley Green's, on Route 44, served Gold Coast Burgers, which consisted of a quarter-pound hamburger covered with cheese and two strips of bacon on a bulky roll. Patrons were tempted 1974-style with homemade desserts, such as Boston Cream Pie and Strawberry Whipped Cream Cake.

On Fall River Avenue at the end of the Interstate 195 Exit 1 off-ramp in Seekonk was Howard Johnson's Restaurant and Motor Lodge. The familiar bright orange roof of both buildings could be seen for a distance away while driving on the highway in the mid-1970s.

"Home of the $2.00 Shoe" was the slogan in 1974 for The Clothes Pin, a woman's wear shop specializing in ladies sportswear at the Briarwood Plaza. The younger crowd frequented the store quite often, as prices were reasonable and fashion was current.

Eileen Darling's Restaurant started out as Dutchland Farms and expanded into a full-scale restaurant. In 1975, it was a popular place to go for Sunday dinner, as well as breakfast or a lighter meal. Mrs. Darling greeted the arriving guests on a regular basis.

Evergreen Tree & Landscape Service Inc. on Oakhill Avenue offered a variety of trees and shrubs in 1975. The garden center has grown throughout the years and offers its current customers a complete array of gardening services.

By 1975, Brennan's Drug Store on Route 6 was filling the prescriptions of many South Seekonk residents. It was a local drug store where the pharmacist, Dennis Flowers, knew each customer and frequently asked, by name, how other family members were doing.

K-Mart, at Route 44 and Fall River Avenue, was the first place many people ventured out to after the Blizzard of '78 travel ban was lifted on February 11, 1978. Snow removed from the parking spaces after this storm was piled up about 15 feet high at the far edge of the lot.

"Only floss the teeth you want to keep." Built in 1985, the dental office of Jared W. Stubbs, D.D.S., is located at the Pine Grove Professional Center on Taunton Avenue, at the Peck Street corner. In addition to traditional preventative and restoration services, the office also offers a full range of cosmetic procedures.

Leonard's Antiques, established in 1933, specializes in furniture. With clientele from around the country, the store rightly emphasized customer satisfaction. Through a large window located at the rear of the store, the customer can watch the cabinet-makers and finishers in the finely equipped woodworking shop performing their craft. Pictured here in 1979 with the owner, Mrs. Hazel Leonard, are Bruno Nigra, David Woodsham, Robert Jenkins (then manager), Doug Miranda, Meyer Spitzman, Jorge Rijo, and Gilbert Barrowclough.

Three

Farms:
Plants and Animals

Seekonk was predominantly a farming community and remained so for years. Neighbors and relatives were always ready to lend a helping hand. Construction of farm buildings and harvest time brought townspeople together in supportive endeavors. In this picture taken at the Toher Florist greenhouse on West Avenue in 1900, the gardener checks his flowering crop. Maintaining constant temperature in the glass structure was difficult, as rays of the winter sun were just as likely to burn plants as those of the summer sun. Each window had to be opened and closed manually, depending on the weather conditions throughout the day, seven days a week.

Two women wearing long skirts stand at the edge of the cabbage patch in 1911. When the cabbages "head up," they will be picked and stored in a cool spot, like the root cellar, for use throughout the winter months.

These farmers took to the task of training twin calves to wear a yoke on this summer day in 1923. Eventually, the team would be able to drag a plow behind them, preparing the fields for planting. Richmond, holding the rope whip, shows the calves who will be in charge.

Ice cutting at the Grist Mill pond in the early 1920s was a tedious job. Each block had to be sawed by hand and carried to the icehouse. Sawdust, acting as an insulation material, was packed around each block to prevent excessive melting as the temperature outside warmed up.

By the mid to late 1920s, ice cutting got easier for the Mellen family. This laborer had the advantage of an electric saw to cut the blocks of ice. Not only was it a time-saver, it also allowed this operation a greater harvest.

An aerial view of the Peck Farm in the late 1920s shows the lay of the land. The rectangular fields have been planted in long rows and show signs of a productive year for the farm. All farm buildings, holding animals and machinery, were relatively close to each other and the farmhouse, with the fields spreading out for acres in all directions.

Looking from the Hopkins family's home at 33 Newman Avenue toward the present reservoir and across to Rumford, Rhode Island, and the Bridgham's farm, this 1929 view shows how the land appeared before the reservoir was flooded in 1935. The glass greenhouse and flower garden were among the many areas covered by water at the completion of the project. Newman Avenue can be seen at the extreme right-hand side of the photo.

The Coyle farmhouse and barns weather out a small snowstorm in the late 1920s. Besides tending to the animals, a farm in the winter months showed little sign of activity outdoors. The acreage covered from Central Avenue to the railroad tracks.

Throughout the late 1920s and early 1930s, Oliver Hopkins raised chickens in his backyard on Newman Avenue. The chickens were kept in a wooden coop, which had a wire mesh screen door. The area they were in was flooded when the reservoir was created.

In 1930, the Jacob's Hill Hunt Club was a thriving horse farm. People from all over the area boarded their horses there and came out to ride them for the fox hunts that were held on a weekly basis in the adjacent trails and fields.

"A woman's work is never done." Mrs. Perrin helps her husband in 1931 by getting behind the plow team and turning over one of the fields, while Mr. Peck tends to more labor intense tasks.

At Peck's Farm, you could always find one or more of the Pecks working in the field. At a rare moment in 1932, J. Wesley Peck Sr., Eugene Peck, and Harold Peck stand near one of the farm vehicles for this group photo.

During the summer of 1935 at the Perrin Farm Stand on Brown Avenue in the North End, passersby could pick out freshly grown produce. Most of the vegetables were sold by the pound and were weighed on the metal scale hanging above the edge of the shelf.

On Easter Sunday morning, April 17, 1938, Mr. DaSilva shows off his twin calves that were born weeks earlier, on March 23. Once full grown, these calves would be used for working the fields, providing food for the family, or breeding purposes.

On Valentine's Day, 1940, the milkman from Stone's Dairy makes a visit to one of the customers on his route. He carries the empty bottles back to his truck in a milk crate. Like the mailman, he delivered in any type of weather.

In the early 1940s, the Berry Farm was considered to have the largest barn in New England. Tasca Lincoln-Mercury, a branch office of Fleet Bank, Johnson & Wales Inn, and the Firefly Golf Course now occupy the acreage.

At the Olney Farm in 1942, a farmer in his denim bib apron checks the leaves and stem of a plant for parasites or flying insects that may have entered the greenhouse through an opened door or from an unchecked potted plant.

A farmer sits high in the seat of his new John Deere tractor, ready to work the newly planted June fields of 1943. The large, rambling grape vineyard supplied a sufficient amount of sun-ripened fruits for making wine.

Fall harvest time, September 19, 1943, brought everyone out working. The horse is hitched up to the cart in anticipation of a load of dried corn to be hauled to the silo for fodder during the winter months.

Visiting from California, Virginia used to spend her summer vacation at her aunt's farm getting reacquainted with her East Coast cousins and country living. In July of 1942, she cultivated the tomato patch that she had planted earlier in the season. The "patch" covered close to an acre in area. By the beginning of August, red, ripe tomatoes were ready to harvest for market.

Irving Dickens (wearing the hat), owner of Belwing Turkey Farm on Taunton Avenue, examines the 1947 Thanksgiving flock with his foreman, William Pimental. As the farm gets busy with customers coming in to pick up their turkeys, Belwing hires traffic police during the holiday week to direct the constant flow of traffic entering and exiting the parking lot at the farm.

Amaral's Chicken Farm (1960) on County Street was a well-known place to purchase fresh chicken or chicken parts on a wholesale or retail level. Mr. Amaral supplied farm-fresh chickens for barbecues held by numerous organizations in the area.

In 1974, Read's Dairy supplied customers with rich Guernsey milk and other dairy products. Read's was forced to reduce the number of routes and home deliveries per week, due to strong competition from grocery and convenience stores. The dairy eventually closed.

Four

Schools:
Students and Staff

Attendance at school was expected of all children. There were exceptions, as a schoolgirl would stay home to tend to younger siblings if the mother was ill or had just given birth. Boys had a valid reason to be absent during haying, planting, and harvest seasons. In this 1900s photograph, a teacher and group of students pose in front of their small, one-room district school, the Walker Street School. Despite the fact that the district schools were on the decline, the town did not construct its first modern schoolhouse until 1911.

The entire 1907 Jacob Street School population poses in front of their white schoolhouse, an oddity in its day as most schools were painted red. Mrs. Whipple, the teacher, can be located in the middle of the back row.

This young man stands on the front lawn of his school in 1914. It would most likely be his first opportunity to share a teacher with children only at his grade level.

The Luther's Corner Grammar School was one of the last district schools in operation. By 1917, it had seen many students enter through its doors, with most children completing their entire school experience in this one building.

Four 1917 schoolmates, Cora Fratus, Mary DaSilva, Marian Tyler, and Elsie Van Valkenburg, from the Luther's Corner School get together on a summery day. Along with the white skirts and overblouses, they had white bows of varying sizes adorning their hairdos.

Pleasant Street School was the third school built in the modern era of the Seekonk School Department. This brick school, which once went up to ninth grade, was the first junior high school that the town had. The school, as it appeared in 1935, closed in the 1980s, but remained an educational facility. It is currently operating as the South Coast Educational Collaborative.

Surrounded by a stone wall, Wheeler School on Walker Street at Prospect Street had a commanding view of its fields. Originally the Daniel Carpenter homestead built in 1806, it underwent many alterations prior to this 1942 scene.

Heterogeneously mixed classrooms of thirty students were quite common at North School in 1956. Some students would leave the room for individual instrumental music lessons, which coincided with the vocal music program.

Miss Sylvia Hall and her 1957–58 fourth-grade class have completed a unit of study pertaining to farming at the former Monroe Corners School on School Street. The Administration Office of the Seekonk School Department is currently housed there.

The North End Grammar and Primary School was the first modern school in Seekonk. Due to increasing population throughout the town in the 1950s, an annex of four classrooms and an all-purpose room were built onto the original six-room school, which is still in use today.

The Newman Avenue School (as it appeared in 1961), or the Mildred H. Aitken School (as it is now known), has provided service to the children of Central Seekonk. Students who live within a mile-and-a-half radius must walk to school, while those living over that distance are allowed to take the bus. To make room for the growing population of youth in town, an addition has been recently completed.

Mrs. Sturke's first graders at Newman Avenue School started the day off with morning prayer in 1961. A student was usually chosen to lead the exercises. Since the U.S. Supreme Court ruling, prayer has been discontinued in the classroom.

This Newman Avenue School third-grade class and their teacher, Mrs. George, visited the school library every Friday during the 1961–62 school year. All the students took turns choosing interesting books to read for pleasure.

Lunchtime for grades five and six at the Pleasant Street School was a time to get caught up on the news of the day, whether receiving a nourishing hot lunch or brown-bagging it from home. In 1961, Seekonk served 169,395 meals and 140,590 bottles of milk.

Adult education classes were held in Seekonk during the early 1960s. While the instructor finished her sketch of a landscape, students sat at long cafeteria tables attempting their own creative masterpieces.

Anne C. Greene School (1962) on County Street was built in 1925 as a replacement for Luther's Corner School, which was about ninety years old. Village Green Preschool currently occupies this site, and area children now go to George R. Martin Elementary School at the intersection of Olney and Anthony Streets. Martin School was built to replace Anne C. Greene School and to accommodate the rising population in the South Seekonk area.

FIRST GRADE

In 1962, Mrs. Clancy's fifth-grade class at Newman Avenue School demonstrated their ability to keep physically fit through moderate exercise. This routine, doing pull-ups or chin-ups, was referred to as "Chin and Grin" by the many students who enjoyed an opportunity to take a break from academic classes and release some of their stored energy during physical education class.

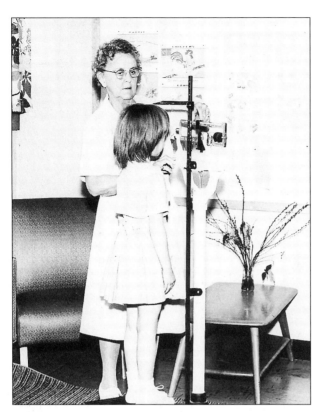

The school nurse, Mrs. Collotta V. Robinson, checks the weight and height of this little girl at North School in 1962. She also checked the hearing and eyesight of each student at regular intervals. Dr. Edwin Viera was the school physician.

Not having a high school of its own, Seekonk sent its older students to out-of-town facilities for their education. By 1965, the building on Arcade Avenue had begun, and the doors to the new high school opened on January 20, 1966.

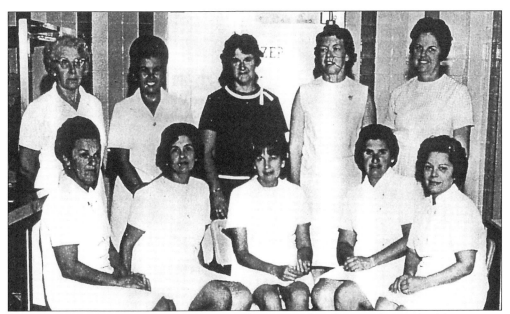

The 1970 Seekonk High School cafeteria staff was up and cooking at the crack of dawn to get lunches prepared for the ravaging teenage appetites that went through the cafeteria lines daily.

The faculty lounge at Seekonk High School was the place to exchange educational concepts and strategies over a bottle of soda. Many of the faculty members at the school in 1970 still teach there today.

All ready for his first day of kindergarten in September of 1986, an excited, five-year-old John J. Wolstencroft prepares to board his yellow school bus. Now that he has his license, Jay drives himself to school. His backpack undoubtedly contained all the ingredients necessary to make a successful kindergarten student: pencil, paper, juice, and snack. His success in the classroom continues to this day.

Frederick Nelson, Omer Leclerc, and Al Goodwin were class advisors in 1974. Both Mr. Nelson and Mr. Leclerc currently assume roles of administrative assistants at Seekonk High School.

The Seekonk High School Class of 1987 showed their enthusiasm at Spirit Week activities. Each year, during the three days preceding Thanksgiving, classes compete for points to see which class has the most spirit.

The Seekonk Memorial Garden was established in 1997 outside of the south lobby of the high school in honor of deceased staff and students. Larry Hindle of Evergreen Tree & Landscape assisted in planting this living tribute.

The Aitken School on Newman Avenue continues to grow, meeting the needs of its students. This 1997 addition includes a new circular-shaped library with numerous windows to allow for natural lighting.

Five

Churches:
Steeples and Peoples

In Seekonk, there are many churches of varying denominations. Each church is unique in its style. A church, however, is not just a building consecrated for worship, for it is the group of worshippers, the congregation, which makes the church what it is. In this picture, the parish of Our Lady of Mt. Carmel Church is celebrating seventy-five years of faith in 1997—"Our Faith is Our Strength." The "new" Mt. Carmel, with a bell tower steeple, was dedicated in a formal religious ceremony on November 21, 1982.

The Seekonk Congregational Church, United Church of Christ (1924), on Fall River Avenue is one of the oldest churches in town. In 1900, the church was raised to build a basement for a hall and Sunday school classes. In 1912, electricity was installed.

The Congregational Church held clambakes, with Isaac Sanford as bakemaster, in the Robinson family's chestnut grove and later in an open field between Belview and Clarke Streets. At this 1920s clambake, men prepare a bed of clams.

A wedding party in the late 1920s posed for this formal outdoor photograph. Included were the bride, her sisters (the four girls in wide-brimmed hats—two standing and two kneeling), the bride's aunt (standing next to the bride), the groom (standing next to his bride), and his groomsmen. White lace, large bouquets of spring flowers, and flowing ribbons added to the ceremony of the day.

On June 21, 1939, Louise A. DaSilva was united in marriage to William Oakland at Our Lady of Mt. Carmel Church by Rev. James E. O'Reilly. Friends and family joined together at a reception before the happy couple left on their honeymoon to Canada.

A boy in knickers and kneesocks poses on June 1, 1941, before heading off to church to receive his first Holy Communion. The ribbon around his upper left arm symbolizes closeness to the heart and his purity and dedication to the Lord on this day.

Located on a triangular piece of land bounded by Newman, Lowell, and Brown Avenues is Seekonk Alliance Church, built in 1959. This church, a member of the Christian and Missionary Alliance, currently has fifty-one members and adherents.

On Easter Sunday, c. 1960, Mrs. Louise DaSilva and her daughter, dressed in their Easter finery, stand in front of a flowering shrub. Hats and gloves were very fashionable, but floral corsages were the finishing touch for each ensemble.

St. Mary's Roman Catholic Church on Coyle Drive was dedicated on May 30, 1957, to satisfy the religious needs of a growing population in the North End. Four majestic columns grace the entry way of the all-white, wooden church. The parish center, located farther down the road on Central Avenue, was completed in the fall of 1970 and serves as a religious education center.

A weather vane sits atop the steeple of The Seekonk Congregational Church. Numerous renovations have been made to the exterior of the church since it was originally built. The most obvious one is that the main entrance is now located at Fall River Avenue. On June 6, 1965, Rev. David Metzler broke ground for Woodward Hall, a religious education center at the rear of the church. Dedication services were held on March 27, 1966.

May 1962 meant First Communion and a May Procession for this seven-year-old girl. Even though the old Mt. Carmel Church no longer stands, memories remain of wooden pews, stained-glass windows, and going to Sunday school, Wednesday night C.C.D., and mass in the church's basement.

Statues of Joseph and the Blessed Mother, Mary, holding Jesus stood on either side of the Mt. Carmel Church altar in this 1971 photograph. The altar piece was placed in the chapel of the new church, as were portions of the stained-glass windows.

On June 8, 1980, Bishop Daniel A. Cronin presided over the Blessing of the Site for the soon-to-be-built Our Lady of Mt. Carmel Church. Rev. Thomas Mayhew, pastor, was joined by other priests and parishioners at the blessing.

Our Lady of Mount Carmel Roman Catholic Church (1982) on Taunton Avenue began as a mission church in 1904. In 1922, the Diocese of Fall River sent Rev. McNamara to serve as pastor of the little brown church.

Faith Christian Center had its beginnings at the Briarwood Plaza on Olney Street. It quickly outgrew the location and in 1985, moved a couple of miles down the road to a beautifully setting with an abundance of trees near a pond on Sagamore Road.

Kingdom Hall of Jehovah's Witnesses is located on Arcade Avenue, directly across the street from Seekonk High School. The blue-gray wooden structure was built in 1986.

In keeping with the motto "The Church that love is building," Faith Christian Center found a need to enlarge and renovate its 1985 site by 1996. This growth allowed even more area for worship, group meeting space, and private conference rooms.

Attached to Faith Christian Center is the Seekonk Christian Academy. The school provides a Christian-based foundation in education for students in kindergarten through grade twelve, where the teacher to student ratio for 1997 was approximately one to ten.

Igreja Evangelica Pentecostal Portuguese Assembly of God Church (1996) is located on Newman Avenue slightly south of Baker's Corner. On nicely landscaped grounds, a steeple-topped entranceway leads one into the white, L-shaped church. On the side of the building is the word "Jesus" with a cross and the Greek symbols for Alpha and Omega linked together—the Beginning and the End.

Located on the northern end of Central Avenue, Route 152, in Seekonk, Memorial Baptist Church of Pawtucket welcomes all to their Sunday worship. The congregation is primarily from Seekonk and Pawtucket, but members also attend from Attleboro and surrounding communities. This 1997 photograph shows the church with its red-bricked front and tall, white columns standing on a grassy incline. A slender, cross-topped steeple reaches skyward.

81

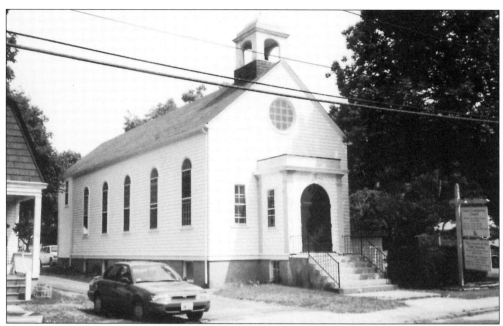

The Church of the Holy Nativity, an Episcopal church, was established in 1923. Grace Community Chapel, which is non-denominational, formed in November 1993 and relocated to Seekonk in 1996. The two separate churches share the same church building on County Street for worship.

During the Summer of 1997, The Free Methodist Church on Taunton Avenue proclaimed, "The Gift of God is Eternal Life" on its signpost facing Route 44. The church has been welcoming residents of Seekonk and area towns since its establishment in 1926.

Six

Government:
Local and Federal

The citizens of the United States of America are provided with a government for the people, of the people, and by the people. Numerous townspeople through different agencies administer or control the affairs of Seekonk. Law and order are the prime concern; however, each department enhances the other—all for the good of the town. In this scene, a brand new 1935 Maxim firetruck is delivered to Seekonk Fire Co. No. 1 on County Street. Carl Lindberg is sitting in the driver's seat with Benjamin Reynolds' dog at his side. The dog was a frequent visitor because he lived next door to the fire station.

Mail delivery in the early 1900s was provided by horse and wagon. Different areas of town were serviced by different post offices. This carrier covered part of the North End of Seekonk and North Rehoboth. It was not until August 1962 that one post office served the entire town.

The first firehouse in town was Fire Co. No. 1 on County Street in 1909. (See current photograph of building in Chapter 7.) The current fire station is located just a few houses up the street on the opposite side of the road.

Proudly standing in front of the fire station displaying their uniforms with the initials LCFCo 1 are members of Luther's Corner Fire Company Number 1. The department came about in 1909, due to residents and merchant W.E. Marcey's concern for safety in the area.

The Baker, Bliss, Carpenter, and Meuberger families were considered founders of Seekonk Fire Department No. 2, built on Pine Street in 1924 to service the North End. To obtain money to build the station, the fire association sold stocks to people in the Baker's Corner area.

By 1928, the town had grown, and the Central Seekonk Volunteer Fire Department was born in the basement of the Newman Avenue School. Members took turns garaging the firetruck at their homes until the station, Fire Co. #3, on Newman Avenue was built.

Seekonk Fire Department #3 was built on Newman Avenue in the 1920s, with Frank Nelson being the first chief. A traffic light has now been placed in front of the station to stop vehicular flow on Route 152 when the fire engines leave the station in response to a call.

Central Seekonk Volunteer Fire
Department Co. #3 set a world record in
the ladder raising event of a firemen's
muster held in Fairhaven, Massachusetts,
on August 1, 1931. It took Francis
Carpenter, Warren Carpenter, Frank
Nelson, and Oscar Gustafson a mere 7.15
seconds to accomplish this feat.

An exuberant 1939 East Providence
High School cheerleader, Shirley Snow,
roots for her football team from the 15
yard line. Shirley Snow Gibson was tax
collector in Seekonk for twenty-five
years before retiring in June 1986. Mrs.
Gibson died in 1995.

On August 16, 1932, the Smart Memorial Library opened on Fall River Avenue, becoming the main library in town. The library was built in memory of Mr. and Mrs. Isaiah Smart by their daughter, Mrs. Isadore Forbes. The brick building was left unattended for some years after it closed. After much restorative work, the former library is now the home of Monterey Corporation.

Robert Woodward, who lived at 500 Woodward Avenue where he ran a dairy, makes an important call on his telephone, c. 1930s. Active in town government, he was the animal inspector in 1917. Mr. Woodward died in October 1955 at the age of ninety-nine.

As Seekonk grew, its post office relocated many times. In the 1940s, the United States Post Office could be found at the corner of Fall River Avenue and lower County Street, where the Exxon Station is presently located. From there, it moved two doors down to a brick building on Fall River Avenue, now a tanning salon.

Asaph C. Hill was active in town politics as a town clerk during the first three decades of the 1900s. He posed for this portrait on November 28, 1942, which was taken by Nelson B. Stackpole, a former Seekonk police chief. Mr. Hill received a salary of $25 for his duties as town clerk when he was first elected. He received an additional salary of just under $30 for licensing purposes.

Parker Dupuoy (pictured here) grew up with his brother Milton in a Newman Avenue home. During World War II, from 1943 to 1945, Parker was an aviator and a member of the Flying Tigers. Upon returning from war, Mr. Dupuoy married his wife, Virginia, and moved 5 miles east to a home in Rehoboth, Massachusetts. There, they raised their family of three children: Susan, Melissa, and Parker Jr.

Carl Lindberg, a land developer who posed for this portrait in 1950, was a selectman during the 1950s and chairman of the finance committee from 1959 to 1963. He remained a member of the finance committee for much of the 1960s.

Sitting behind his desk in 1955, Oliver Hopkins Jr. was ready to serve the people of Seekonk. As a police officer for the Seekonk Police Department, he was usually the only patrolman on the road for the midnight to 8 am shift.

Seekonk used to hold open town meetings such as this one in the 1960s. By the 1970s, representative town meetings were held because there had been a switch from a strong Republican town to one which had competition from other parties.

The 1962 school committee discussed financing costs of renovating, repairing, and equipping schools through capital improvement projects. A study committee stressed that the town build its own high school in order to control the educational program at all grade levels.

The Postal Reorganization Act of 1970 transformed the Post Office Department into a government-owned corporation, the United States Postal Service. In the spring of 1971, the Seekonk Post Office moved to a new and larger facility on Taunton Avenue to serve the public.

On August 2, 1974, a portion of the foundation for Seekonk Commons, a building for the physically handicapped and elderly in town, was poured. Federal Revenue Funds were used to build the seventy-two low-cost housing units on Chappel Street, near Luther's Corner.

Sunday, February 15, 1981, was opening day for the much awaited Seekonk Public Library on Newman Avenue. Money for the project was made available through Federal Reserve Funds in the 1970s. However, the library did not open immediately because there was concern of a methane gas build-up in the building caused by the proximity of the library to an old landfill.

Sergeant Ronald Charron is the D.A.R.E. (Drug Abuse Resistance Education) officer. During his 1997 visits to the elementary schools, he talked to students about resisting drugs and violence. The D.A.R.E. car is a silent but visible reminder to all.

The Seekonk Town Hall (1997) is set on a 20-acre parcel of land located on Peck Street. This municipal office complex opened on November 30, 1977, after being moved from its Taunton Avenue location, the current headquarters of the police department.

Seven
Organizations:
Clubs and Groups

Organizations give people of different backgrounds a common bond to share. Belonging to an organization offers each member an opportunity to meet in an environment that they feel is pleasurable and satisfying. In this above photograph, the four-hour, 10-mile, Sunday "drag hunt" at Jacob's Hill Hunt Club in the 1920s meandered through woods and fields around Pine, Walker, Read, and Prospect Streets. A rider left before the hunt began, dragging a sack soaked in fox urine behind him. The remainder of the group, on horseback, and their beagles would then be in pursuit of this "fox." Upon conclusion of the hunt, members met for a meal and an evening of socialization.

The 1916 Seekonk Mothers' Club was a forerunner of the current day P.T.A. (Parent-Teacher Association). Since its onset, this group has assisted with fund-raisers, organized field trips, and provided support services to schools, teachers, and students.

Seekonk Grange #341 had 114 original, chartered members who met in each other's homes to address social and political needs of the farmer and his family, prior to obtaining their hall at 38 Anthony Street in December of 1924.

Ready to go down the Ten Mile River in the summer of 1917 are Oliver Hopkins, in the third canoe from the right, and other members of the Canoe Club. Many people relaxed on weekends by navigating down the clean, sparkling waters of the river or just lazily, paddling about on Central Pond, enjoying each other's company and the bright sunshine of the day.

This singing group of the early 1930s performed at various organizations around the community. The men and women raised their voices, filling halls with joyful medleys of the times. Many members also sung in church choirs on Sunday mornings.

A group of boys organize a "pick-up" game of football in the field beside the Dupuoy house on Newman Avenue in 1938. Some of the boys wore protective leather helmets, but others just played in their regular street clothes.

Members of the Seekonk Grange stand in front of their meeting hall in the 1940s, where they met on the second and fourth Thursday of every month. One of their most influential and politically active members, Jessie Gray, also served as town moderator.

The magician, Revilo Snikpoh (Oliver Hopkins spelled backwards), pulled a scarf out of his hat at a 1948 performance. Mr. Hopkins was in vaudeville from 1915 to 1920 and performed for organizations such as P.T.A.s, churches, and scouts, until his death in 1964.

At the police department's 1954 Christmas display at Bill Skeese's Restaurant on Newman Avenue opposite Brook Street, Rudolph lights the way for the sleigh filled with warm wishes from Peg, Susan, Stephen, Robert, and Oliver Hopkins Jr. Members of the police department volunteered their time for a few hours each night during the holiday season to take photographs for families to keep or send to loved ones across the country.

Wendy Wolfe, in her Brownie uniform, waits to go into the old Newman Avenue School after an outdoor assembly in the spring of 1956. During the 1990s, Wendy Wolfe-Cardarelli was elected to serve on the board of selectmen in Rehoboth, Massachusetts.

Cub scouts, like Brownies and Girl Scouts, wore their uniforms to school because meetings were held at the end of the school day. In good weather, members were able to go outside and explore their surroundings, using skills learned at den meetings.

A Girl Scout troop performs at a 1956 springtime assembly with musical accompaniment by classmates on bugles. Members of this Girl Scout troop rehearsed their singing for the event at troop meetings, usually held on a weekly basis.

With the population of Seekonk growing steadily through the 1950s and Pleasant Street School becoming more crowded, Seekonk Junior High School was built on Route 152, Newman Avenue. By 1958, a football team was formed to compete against area schools.

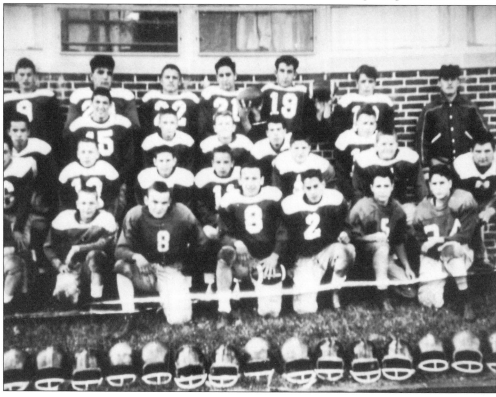

The Seekonk Fire Company #3 on Newman Avenue held annual clambakes to raise money for the department and bolster a sense of community in the neighborhood. At the 1958 clambake, a lady tempted the photographer with juicy clams dipped in drawn butter.

Proudly holding the Seekonk Junior High School banner are two members of the marching band. The group, posed in front of the school in the early 1960s, was directed by Mrs. Sternlight, the woman standing in the front row on the left-hand side.

In the early 1960s, Stephen Hopkins of Newman Avenue became the first Eagle Scout in Seekonk's Boy Scout Troop 3. His younger brother Robert, who was also a member of the troop, looks over the badges that Stephen had received throughout his years in the Boy Scouts of America. Both boys worked hard to earn their badges and were very proud of their accomplishments.

The first pupil shelter built in Seekonk helped protect students from the elements while waiting for the school bus. On January 2, 1962, this shelter, courtesy of the Seekonk Lions Club, kept these youngsters comfortable until the bus arrived.

The first cross country team at Seekonk High School had eight members. From 1967 to 1997, the teams have grown in number, developing into strong competition, breaking league records, and bringing home numerous awards for their achievements.

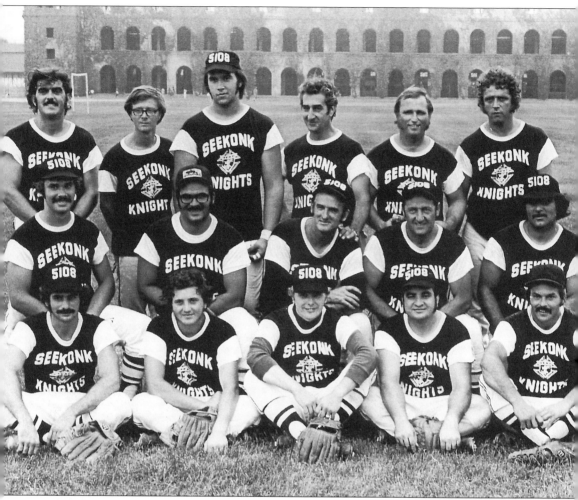

The Seekonk Knights of Columbus Council #5108 won the 1973 State Softball Championship at Harvard Stadium, beating a more experienced Boston group. The Knights of Columbus meet regularly at the Knights of Columbus Hall located on Arcade Avenue, near the intersection of Route 44. The hall was formerly a stop for stagecoaches passing through the area on their way to Jacob's Hill Hunt Club or other locations.

The 1973–74 Seekonk High School basketball team compiled a record of eleven wins and five losses. Under Coach Carey's leadership, the team went on to play in the state basketball tournament, but lost to Westwood by a score of 96–81.

In conjunction with the 1976 Bicentennial Year of the United States of America, Seekonk organized a road race. Hundreds of people competed in this sanctioned run through the town, and hundreds more lined the roadsides to cheer on their favorite runner.

The Newman YMCA ribbon-cutting ceremony was held in 1980 at its new location on Taunton Avenue. In 1985, the swimming pool was opened to meet the needs of a growing membership. Since then, the building has also added a gym and additional equipment.

A gloved Sarah Wolstencroft bends down and fields the ball during a 1989 Seekonk softball league game. Even though the base runner, Erin Durkay, loses her cap, she appears to be safe at second base. It is unknown which team won the game.

American Legion Post #311, now located on Fall River Avenue, was chartered in 1934 and moved into this building in 1948. Before 1948, the American Legion Hall was located on Arcade Avenue. In 1996, the Post dedicated the current hall to Army veteran Richard F. Stockwell for what he had done for the Post and the American Legion at the local, state, and national levels.

On a Cub Scout camping trip in 1990, John Wolstencroft and his son Jay get settled in for an adventurous night of "roughing it" outdoors. The scouts and their dads learned about nature, first aid procedures, and survival skills in the wild.

Located on County Street, the Seekonk Masonic Building, pictured here in 1997, also served as the home of the Luther's Corner Fire and Improvement Association, Seekonk's first volunteer fire department within its modern-day borders.

Seven

Transportation:
Wheels and Drivers

People living in the twentieth century need "wheels" to get around. From baby carriages to public transportation, all vehicles had wheels and drivers. Accessibility to a vehicle provides the operator independence, which was important in a town where traveling to visit or to get supplies was a necessity of life. In this picture taken in the early summer of 1918, baby Richmond DaSilva gets some fresh country air with his first view of Seekonk from his stylish baby carriage. He was the pride and joy of a family already blessed with five daughters.

At the Carpenter House in 1900, this horse and buggy awaits its bearded passenger. Many townspeople traveled from home to home in this manner, as it was quicker than walking and very economical, unless a spoke broke off from the hub of the wooden wagon wheel.

The horse and wagon of D. Lanoie stands at the blacksmith shop in the early 1900s. Here, the village farrier forms custom-made horseshoes for his clients' horses. The young man holding the reins of the white horse is an apprentice at the shop.

At Perrin's Crossing, a railroad station on Pine Street, this young boy stands with his hand placed upon the seat of a handcar. In the 1920s, the station's main use was as a freight stop; however it was used by older students who rode the train daily to attend high school in Providence, Rhode Island. Railroad tracks are still embedded in the roadway on Pine Street.

Amazingly, not one passenger was injured in this January 5, 1921 trolley car crash through the side wall of the Ten Mile River Bridge, although there was major damage to the car and structure. This accident inconvenienced riders of the Interstate Trolley Railway because the lines had to be completely cleared and the bridge fully repaired and tested before travel could be resumed.

In the summer of 1922, this little farm boy, wearing a wide-brimmed hat, rests in his wagon. At four years of age, he was old enough to do some chores around the farm, such as gathering eggs from the hen house and picking vegetables from the fields.

A toddler receives a ride on the back of his older friend's tricycle in 1928. Living in rural Seekonk afforded these two pals the pleasure of wide-open fields to explore, while still remaining within the sight of a watching parent or older sibling.

In 1928, Benjamin Ladd Cook drove the "Liberty," a stagecoach, at the Jacob's Hill Hunt Club. Mr. Cook, the first Master of the Hunt, scheduled the days, determined the route, and supervised the paneling of stone walls and erecting the ramps for the hunt.

The 1935 Seekonk School Department school bus and driver went over bumpy, dirt roads on its route around town each day. This bus also carried its older students to area high schools for their advanced education.

Wearing her full-length fur coat on a cold March 19, 1939, Mary DaSilva was ready for a drive in her black coupe to visit friends in another part of town. Since public transportation did not extend out to her property line, she had the option to either stay at home and rely on others to pick her up when she wanted or needed to go someplace or get a license and a car and go where she pleased, when she pleased.

Automobile accidents tend to happen more frequently in bad weather and at intersections. This fender-bender occurred at the intersection of Newman and Arcade Avenues after a March 1941 snowstorm. As the drivers and passengers collect information for their insurance claims, a young Oliver Hopkins Jr. investigates the damage. This was not to be the only accident that Mr. Hopkins investigated because he eventually became a police officer.

The only way to travel on July 2, 1939, for this young man was on his well-equipped bicycle with dual headlights. From the looks of his appearance, his clothing gives an indication that he was probably on his way to court a girl down the road.

The Interstate Transit Corp. bus was used to carry passengers between Attleboro, Massachusetts, and Pawtucket, Rhode Island. In 1941, this bus made numerous stops daily at Baker's Corner, as well as occasional stops at other locations in the North End.

On his homemade, makeshift snowplow, a John Deere tractor, Richmond DaSilva prepared to keep the road open during a February 10, 1945 snowstorm. The tractor was fitted with wooden attachments connected to the rear axle and a plow in its front, which was permanently fixed at an angle to push the snow farther out of the driveway at each pass. This was an excellent example of Yankee ingenuity.

Two dump trucks met while going in opposite directions over the railroad tracks at the old wooden-planked bridge on Newman Avenue in 1949. With the truck on the left carrying a full load of sand, the combined weights of the two trucks quite possibly exceeded the posted legal maximum load limit of eight tons. The Ellis Wescott home, a white house, can be seen at the right in the photograph.

Anthony Vendetti, owner of Seekonk Speedway, advertises the establishment in 1956. Flooding the oval and using it for speedboat racing was one event which did not catch on with the public. Car racing, however, has continued there for over fifty years.

Bove Motors, a Texaco Service Station at the corner of Lake Street and Route 44, provided sales, service, and parts to its customers through the late 1950s. The building became home to both the Seekonk Police and Public Works Departments until 1978. Since then, the Public Works Department has utilized the entire building.

Mrs. Oldrid's fourth-grade class at North School won the P.T.A. banner for over five consecutive months in the early 1960s. A bus trip, sponsored with P.T.A. funds to Cinerama, a posh movie theater on Hope Street on the East Side of Providence, Rhode Island, was the winning prize for the group. The entire class got dressed up for this special occasion.

This is the way Seekonk Speedway on Route 6 appeared in 1962. The smell of burning rubber from tires and car exhaust meant one thing—racing season had begun. Nonstop racing action on banked asphalt tracks drew crowds from all over the region.

These public school bus drivers for the town of Seekonk in 1973–74 are grouped in front of one of their vehicles. They are the men and women who got the students to school on time each day of the year regardless of weather conditions.

The Blizzard of '78, producing 34 inches of snow in thirty-four hours, stopped traffic for almost five days. Seekonk Police borrowed snowmobiles from townspeople as cruisers, and emergency vehicles were not able to navigate over snow-filled roadways like Route 44.

The winning 1985 Homecoming float at Seekonk High School was loaded with elated and energetic teenagers, who spent hours decorating for their annual event. Homecoming Weekend is filled with activities such as a home-scheduled football game and dance.

New 1997 cars and used cars can be found at dealerships or lots throughout the entire town of Seekonk. In approximately a 1-mile stretch of Route 44 from the East Providence, Rhode Island, state line heading east, a new (1997) or used car shopper can visit dealerships which carry Chrysler-Plymouth, Hyundai, Isuzu, Lincoln-Mercury, Honda, and Saturn products. The Route 6 area also provides shoppers with a vast array of automobile services.